Paralogues

Evan Jones was born in Toronto. A dual citizen of Canada and Greece, he has lived in Britain since 2005. He has a PhD in English and Creative Writing from the University of Manchester and has taught at York University in Toronto, and in Britain at the University of Bolton and Liverpool John Moores University. His first collection, *Nothing Fell Today But Rain* (2003), was a finalist for the Governor General's Literary Award for Poetry. He is co-editor of the anthology *Modern Canadian Poets* (Carcanet, 2010).

T0096346

Also by Evan Jones from Carcanet Press

Modern Canadian Poets: An anthology of poems in English
(with Todd Swift)

New Poetries V: An Anthology (contributor)

EVAN JONES

Paralogues

CARCANET

First published in Great Britain in 2012 by
Carcanet Press Limited
Alliance House
Cross Street
Manchester M2 7AQ

A CIP catalogue record for this book is available from the British Library

ISBN 978 1 84777 137 7

The publisher acknowledges financial assistance from Arts Council England

Typeset by XL Publishing Services, Tiverton
Printed and bound in England by SRP Ltd, Exeter

For my parents

All the incongruous things of past incompatible ages…
Arthur Hugh Clough

Acknowledgements

Some of these poems have appeared in the journals *Agni, Antigonish Review, Kaffeeklatsch, Malahat Review, Manchester Review, New Quarterly, New Walk, PN Review, Poetry Review, Poetry Wales, The SHOp, Southwest Review, The Wolf,* and in the anthologies *Lung Jazz: Young British Poets For Oxfam* (Cinnamon Press, 2012) and *New Poetries V* (Carcanet, 2011). My thanks to Jason Guriel, John McAuliffe, Jena Schmitt and Norm Sibum for early readings of the poems and manuscript.

Contents

Self-portrait with Argus the Hundred-Eyed

Many-eyer, many-eyer, many heroes
      are dull, children of Dutch
millionaires, sons of Prussian princes,
      who bear the names
of champagnes known the world over;
      and through our fifty-one
telescopes we glimpse the moon,
      the stars, and Venus,
when the clouds clear long enough,
      all unimportant but present,
a manageable version of the evenings
      wasted herding and flocking,
while you could take a city single-handed,
      you could go to the dogs,
or otherwise turn up your toes – sing
      here we are again! –
the moon presiding over the chestnut tree
      and then beyond it,
the acacia losing a leaf to the wind:
      all this behind you now.

Little Notes on Painting

Take a Spanish painter and put him in Paris. Take a Greek
painter and put him in Madrid. Take a Quebeçois painter
and put him in Paris, too, and a German and a couple
more Spaniards and also a Greek-born Italian. You wouldn't
believe what I'm doing now. I'm up very late. I'm placing
an American painter in Albany and hoping school
will be cancelled tomorrow. There are fewer and fewer days
like this left; they fall like uses for wax paper. Don't ever
mention abstract artists to my face or my books, my friend, for
who owns a house and has never been kissed in one? Right?
Take a Russian painter and put him in New York beside
a Mexican painter. I am two feet from the bed; the pillows
and blankets are swelling and rising towards the ceiling.
Take a Javanese painter and put him in Cairo.
The phone won't ring anymore. I called a street artist
'Picasso' but thought better of it as all those women were
going down on him one at a time and bearing him children.
Take a little-known Nova Scotia folk painter and put her,
posthumously, in Cleveland or Skopjë. The mattress is filling
with honey and the box spring is humming like bees; my hand is
in my pyjama bottoms. I stop and say, it isn't love
that makes you weak, to the night table or maybe the bed frame.
Take an Italian Futurist for example. Take a nineteenth-century
Japanese print and slip it between the mattress and the box spring.
Take a pregnant painter by the hand. I'm home and touching
the unborn child of her easel. It would be nice for a night
if silence was the colour of water but it would be nicer
to sleep in the desert. Take a stolen Brueghel from
the Kunsthistorisches Museum, Vienna, and bury it
on Easter Island. I arrange the sheets every morning
to resemble Mount Athos so that every night I sleep
on God's arm. What did I say about abstraction?
Take a British painter from a home he's not once ever loved
and ask him why he never paints the same thing. Take a moment
to join an art school, the aristocracy or merely buy
a beret. A photograph of a painter's palette is no good to
anyone and the sky outside is nothing like Van Gogh.
I just wanted to say that the moon's going down.
I remember every moment. Thank you.

Portrait (Artist's Model, Sleeping Nude)

Naturally, what I should have done I did not do.

You may recognise a young woman unaffected by
catalepsy, a woman who can crane her neck,
a woman who can swan, who can duck, swallow,
and thrush. Her image is unfinished, unrealised,
but my intention was always to get away from myself.
As with anything, I must change her, change her
skinny legs, change her cold greyness into butterflies –
something never around when I think of them.
Do I truly reveal these secrets to you?
The canvas was never meant to be all in all.

She is sitting for three months, three times a week, and never
coming late. Possible reasons for this include:
a) the need for a friendship she can turn to without shame or
sense of desperation b) flattering remarks
c) the sight of a paintbrush with all the fur eaten by a moth
d) jungle plants that eat people e) the climate of the Pyrenees.
The strongest influence is possibility.

You ask about technique and composition:
one is the business of human beings and one is not.
Neither have to do with you, so don't ask again.
The door and chair are less obvious, I agree.
Yet the bird's nest and broken glass should be
satisfactorily symbolic. As well, the gull,
about to poetically take to the wind before rainfall,
is an eyesore but I would be sad were it gone.
Everything must be here, in mind.

That other artist who sculpted her shriking or toucaning,
I can't be certain – as long as I live I'll never appreciate it.
It has no sense of rest. She may, I often wonder
during a session, go to sleep with her head on my lap.
Notice that I've never mentioned opportunity. So let me
think this then and not wonder a moment longer.

Today? In my mouth and heart everything is bitter.

Mr. Eugenides, the Smyrna Merchant

1

'Once, when I asked him to lunch,'
reported Mr. Eugenides, 'he cracked up,'
unshaven, with a pocket full of currants,
his thin-nostrilled, Turanian nose twitching.
'For all his charms and faults, fair grooming,
this was years ago, we could have a good time.'
He knocked his salad fork to the floor,
gathered it with grit and hair into his sticky fingers.
'Friends? No and yes. He was someone
who could be asked too much of.'
He put the fork into his satchel,
the brown one always by his side,
in which he also kept notebook and pens.
He was avoiding the maître d', the waiters,
had ordered only appetisers and a cup of tea.
'Back then, there wasn't as much of civilization.
He preferred it.' He kicked the table leg,
but then changed his mind. 'I'm only saying,
a wet stone drying in the sun, here and gone.'

2

'Looking to the sea wall, I caught sight
of a horse,' his story continued,
from memory, from sharpness of pain.
'It was on fire, was chasing wildly
across the quayside, trampling children,
its hindquarters engulfed in flames.'
Our second meeting, he, in khaki chinos
and a striped Oxford, in showing trust,
shaved, washed, let me buy him lunch.
'Here was the horse, determined' –
he dropped his drinking glass
and covered the table with cola –
'going up to heaven pulling its chariot of fire.'
Our waiter delivered cloth napkins,
fumbled a half-smile and slipped away.
'This was 14 September 1922.
A month later I was back in London,
rid of friends and any relations.
Yes, his poem was in *The Criterion*:
we never spoke after that.'

Letter to Sofia

At that time, I was ignorance,
ignorance in running shoes.
Later on, I was a pullman
coasting past border guards,

detained only by you, Sofia.
I found your theatres and restaurants empty,
your windows blank eyes,
your blackbirds frozen in the air.

In you, the streets were always distant,
no matter where I stood, and warm,
red light shone out of every church door –
though the thought of worshippers still astounds.

In you, the seasons were suspended,
the sky, the anonymous people.
I had been, I admit, an architect
in these matters, sleeping, staring,

the mountains behind me – always
too far to reach. But I was always
trying to reach you, even on nights
it was difficult to rest,

and when word arrived that the Black Sea
no longer rolled in to the shore
at Varna, I knew all those cold, sad
Bulgarians were losing sight of their goals

and heading for the mountains in despair.
Future victims of suicide?
I couldn't be certain. The cold wasn't
so terrible. Some faced it

with a desire to be tortured,
taking up the urge to hold
a former lover's hand, as if
in yielding to it, declaring affection

for it, pretending it existed
somehow made the winter seem more
significant than a flight of
pigeons or a field of macchie.

Sofia, could you tell the lovers in you
one thing beyond their own deaths? Tell them
I see them. When the moon goes down
behind the trees I imagine

the parts of their bodies that others'
fingers might have been inside.
And while it may occur to you
that I am writing here about loss,

I swear I'm not. I will wander
the Earth for as long as it takes you
to understand. For you, Sofia,
lover till death of mountains and loss.

Cavafy in Liverpool

Here is your sad young man:
he is ship-to-shore, he is buttoned-down
in tweed and scarved, eyes closed
when the Mersey wind

calls his collar to his ear
on the strand near Albert Dock,
some January, some winter day
we recognize but take no part in.

Here is your boy at the end of the shore
while the waters continue
touching place and nothing,
hold something dear and don't,

the desire and devotion
to an island he never dreams.
Not summoned, not answered,
he searches the world growing dim

as the river swells and recedes,
like closed eyelids shifting during sleep.
One less wave, he thinks, one less,
and then the Persians can get through.

The Intercity Express Passes Günzburg

after Robert Gernhardt

Günzburg, the many-steepled:
we bypass Günzburg once more,
a venerable city,
but the train doesn't stop here.

In fact:

If just once the train did stop –
would I have gotten off there?
That I know nothing of Günzburg
isn't down to schedule and fare.

Because:

Dread can lock a man in place:
approaching beauty can take years.
Doesn't everyone know this?
So when Günzburg appears –

But:

No one sets foot in Günzburg.
None offer Günzburg a care.
No one, afire in the light,
suffers over Günzburg in dark.

Because:

If something holds onto us,
we can't take it in our arms.
Which suggests just one conclusion:
see Günzburg from the train.

And not only Günzburg.

Sheep or Llama

for Marion

What we're looking at, through this forest of whitened wood,
over the slope there, where the country's gone quiet,
is matte and grey and just about anything.

When it begins to sing, surprising us, between
gnawing at grass and hedge, we're taken in its song,
called to mind a winter beyond our own:

a moonless night in December, where we, two creatures
in parkas, take up another's sad music,
beyond the trees, the snow, the end of days.

At the back fence, out of sight but not hearing,
we can't be sure if it is sheep or llama,
but our matters are vision and its are sullen.

Burgau to Ulm, Bundesland Bavaria

Two foxes hefted the remains of a pigeon,
within the shadow of an onion-domed steeple,
and from the train's window, watching: you, me, no one,

mooning the winter through, wishing work to be done,
holding out for bits of money like most people –
like a fox hefting the remains of a pigeon

that had landed to rest its wings and lost everyone.
We're there now, holding the scene, an example
in our heads, a window through which you, me, no one,

can view your childhood home, the thin, scrambled sun,
and the sickness that drives you to sleep. Our couple –
as two foxes heft the remains of a pigeon,

dragging and chomping bits of bird to fill their own,
the world just darker, colder – rest a little
within the train's window. There's you, me, and no one,

all failing to arrive on time at the station,
our lives framed against the February chill,
where two foxes heft the remains of a pigeon
while watching, as a train passes, you, me: no one.

Bundesland Bavaria, between Deffingen and Denzingen

Between Deffingen and Denzingen,
      summer opened the road
forward, browning the fields and hillsides
      of a country so barren
that the smallest horse grazing seemed
      resentful and withdrawn:
no longer seat-and-throne-of-men
      but pigeon-grey splotch
on the *Blaue Reiter* landscape, inured
      forever to the flow
of traffic, where once it drank from rivers,
      and aware of itself
as fodder for the glue factory,
      as much cattle as the cattle.
Between the route the Neckar runs
      and the dirty Danube,
neither the chatter of nits nor
      the bleatings of birds
on the horse's chest, its spreading ears
      folding over the wind
as night comes on. Stones and woods
      stay no longer in their places,
begin to course, sing and wheel,
      like livestock once did,
leaving behind the parcel of the world
      over the larded breast
of Southern Germany: a resource,
      a wind through which
the horse rolls up to heaven
      its dull and stolid eyes.

God in Paris, 1945

Since the world ended He had been living
there, coming and going along the length
of the trembling Champs Élysées. Free
of the stars and prayer, His work tragically

out of fashion, the old city had seemed
as good a place to wander as any
and so, being wandering itself,
and swarming solitude, He paced along

the cobbled streets like a child lost in peat moss.
The Germans were gone, Céline with them,
and Jean Lumière singing '*Faisons Notre
Bonheur Nous-Mêmes*' in cafés stung His ears.

'Either the universe is infinite
or I am,' He remarked to passersby,
'Either the universe is finite or
I am. Or I'm not. Or I'd better be.'

If you reached out to touch His hand, even
accidentally, you will remember Him.
For your hand is stone while your eyes and hair
are the wind that opens and shuts my book,

an ocean and sixty years away from
His room in the Hôtel du Marais, third
arrondissement, an unknowable land.
O rise wind, take my scattered pages

to vast and empty Paris. Either God lies
in a bed of earth alongside all
of history's dead or He doesn't. Or He'd
better. Whatever way wind, don't let up.

Santorini

Certain days pass without a word between us,
where we walk in the street, always near the caldera
and she is younger than ever, pony girl, little donkey.

And in the nights following our days of walking
in silence, the world becomes shaped like a leaf
or a feather instead of always seeming so round.

The mornings that follow may be full of words
but these are unwelcome or maybe even unrecognizable
because so much has been said but not between us.

Our dream is to live here in this moment.
The road that begins near the museum curves up
as we walk, our feet becoming heavier, and 'Tell me,'

one of us thinks, 'do you ever want some company,
or someone to make you dinner and breakfast?
So much time has passed in this way for others.'

Our dream is to live here in this moment, side by side
and walking in silence always along the caldera,
past busy cafés, expensive restaurants,

hotels, blue-domed churches, whitewashed houses and stores,
the light insisting along with the air that there
is no way to continue, to travel deeper.

But we find our way. The road winds past a store
selling postcards and if one of us thought,
'I could reach the sea from here,' we would jump,

not because either is anxious to die but because
one would follow the other, prince or princess of lilies.
And to rise from the foam, clotheless, her skin all orange

and mine all brown – all eager to leave us behind –
and our eyes, peacock's eyes, filling with the sea
and salt and feathers. To live here in this moment

while trying not to repeat ourselves, walking
and looking down over the ocean, bodies built on top of bodies,
where all these things will be dust soon and are dust now.

When we reach the highest point we care to reach,
'Let's go,' one of us thinks, 'we might walk down
not up this next time or else not bother jumping.'

Or we might at last take each other,
our dream of living in this moment over,
she in her short pants and I in my vestments,

the smell of pine trees everywhere.

The Devoted Widow

In an obscure and likely apocryphal aside
in his *Secret History*, Procopius reminds us
of the death and unstitching of Domitian,
Vespasian's son, the carved one
for whom murder wasn't final enough.
His wife Domitia requested the body,
the pieces anyway, resolved to bury it
and carry out a coup against the inhuman court.
When she succeeded in gathering his flesh,
the widow of Domitian, Emperor of Rome,
ordered the whole sculpted in bronze,
the only extant monument,
erected in the street leading
to the Capitol: the visage and the end.

Justinian's Advisors Recall Him Prophesying

He told how in his dream he had pictured
us standing somewhere in Byzantium,
opposite Chalcedon, pushing the shore
forward, heaping stones to rival the strength

of the sea – which sounds empty, and rightly,
dreamed from the lower reaches of nature.
(Not that we criticized, for our true Lord upon
the Golden Horn knew better his nature.)

When we'd run out of rock, there were bodies,
the victims, their crutches, slings, splints, wheelchairs –
the whole lot of our wounded lives, it seems,
spread there and surfacing over the horizon.

We nodded along at every detail,
took notes, wondered if the next time he would
sleep through until the Lord took him, and we,
no further than war's edge, were free from blame.

Journey

after Miltos Sachtouris

When I was walking up the street
and the moon burned my hands
the baker's daughter the owl would awaken
then I'd go out and call the Night

When I was wading down the river
the tanner had nowhere to sleep
her secret wounded me in the chest
then I'd go out and call the Night

When I was going up the stairs
and quails were tangled in my toes
and pulling a man by his hair
then I'd go out and call the Night

When I was going down the stairs
and roses were growing in the sink
waiting there for me to speak
then I'd go out and call the Night

And when I'd take to the street again
and iron grew from the ground
and any gratitude writhed in blood
then I'd go out and call the Night

Three Actaeons

1

Some names are words for grief,
graceless words for failure.
Actaeon was a crowd, a lonely man,
and in the end nothing,
awaiting his descent into simple witlessness,
cold beside a river of fire, who,
the story goes, either wandered
into a grove sacred to Artemis
and saw her bathing naked
or boasted he was the greater hunter.

And so, enduring the deep wrath of god,
thinking, *No way out of this,*
about to surrender, it came to him that,
like any hound or creature in this world,
he too had yearned and hunted.

Later on in the underworld, he would wonder
about symmetry, his cousin, unborn heirs
to the throne of Cadmus and whether or not
he'd been forgiven: a crowd, a lonely man,
nothing, awaiting his descent into witlessness,
and so cold near Phlegethon,
boundless river of fire.

Some men have grief in place of dreams.
How cold and sad an end those men will come to:
white caps over the blue, no linden trees
or red acorns under which to find shade,
and not one god to pray for mercy to.

2

Cy Twombly's Death of Actaeon *(1962/63)*

Now the dogs are loud and black. Now what should
be blood and skin is yellowing as a fire fighting to ignite

everywhere yellows at its edges. There is no wind in the trees,
no wild heavens, no movement but on the earth. We find

ourselves at the end of a story, past the stumbling into
sin, beyond the transgression or whatever it is sets a goddess off.

Artemis, dressed in dignity and sanity, is gone, left before
the finale. Yes. Here it comes: the forest full of black dogs,

loud but not barking, and Actaeon, their teeth in his seams, horns
held high, belling out their names. Well, she knew how it would end.

3

after Raoul Schrott

Yesterday at noon thin cypress shadows raking
the sun over the hills you ascended the stairs
at the house passing me with fewer than no words
and in the way your hair moved I noticed
sensed that something was different
there was only one look I expected nothing
and followed you – your sandals in the hallway
where you slipped out of your dress carefree
your leather purse on the tile – I didn't
bend myself down to it but instead
pushed the door to the shower open slowly – you sang out
in a shrill falsetto and I stared at you how you
over my back small
hands over blushing breasts then
knew you'd been with another man
that you stood more naked than I or the world
would ever find you your hair dripping water
onto your clavicles and wrapping
itself round you like a net – speak say what you have to say
that I while hunting
for the same had surprised you and cut out
my tongue – your fingers flicked water at me hard
like rain in the face and I sank to my heels
truth a broken mirror
shame an invisible wound
hounds panting in the grass below clawed at each other
their barking such that it fed itself into the heat.

How I Became one of my Poems

This is the story of ——, who woke one morning in her bedroom to the sound of dogs barking and realized that her body was the same shape as Ubu's in Max Ernst's portrait, wrote the young novelist who had decided she wanted to write something clever. Her previous attempt, which was a story itself in first person starring a young woman who fell in love with a man who resembled Ubu in Max Ernst's portrait himself had led her nowhere and a decision was made after two weeks of starts and mis-starts to abandon the premise and begin anew. The first clue to being clever, she decided, was to make every *thing* resonate. She would begin, for instance, with that first sentence. Did Ubu have a dog? She didn't know; she had never read the play and only knew the painting by Max Ernst from a catalogue she had seen in a bookstore near her house. The colour plate was cold and dark but she knew she, herself, would be very entertained by a lover who spun like a top and so the decision to write the story. How did one realize upon waking up that one's body had become a spinning top? she thought to herself sitting over the keyboard. Perhaps the realization was one that a young woman must come to over the course of the story, she concluded, and so rewrote the first sentence, leaving out the dogs as well. This is the story of ——, who woke one morning. She stopped. What was the initial impetus for including dogs? she wondered. Although at night she had often heard barking dogs, it was rare that one woke her and so where had the idea come from that barking dogs might wake her character. She froze and stared out the window. Her apartment had a view over the city facing south towards the water but with the haze of the day she couldn't see very far out. This is the story of ——, she wrote. She had still not decided on a name for her character either. In clever books, names always resonate, she thought, but in what way? For instance, she knew from the front of the catalogue that Max Ernst had been involved with other painters, many women. But Leonora and Dorothea sounded ridiculous and far too mid-century and Meret was just too foreign. If she called her character Carrie Tanning, Carrie for Leonora Carrington and Tanning from Dorothea but Tanning sounded too upper class New York American to her. Like a store where one bought chandeliers, Tanning's on Fifth. And then backed with Carrie, which was too southwestern Ontario in its way, to her, or maybe even rang with a Stephen King-ish tone. This is the story of, she wrote. Maybe the beginning was too clever, she thought. Who starts stories with 'This is the story of' and thinks adults will read it? But she had not read enough Doris Lessing to be able to answer that question. A lover who spins like a top, she thought to herself, how would she love him? Her hands fell away from the keyboard to her sides. The horizon was not getting clearer through her window. She stood up from her chair and pushed it in until it clacked against her desk. She began to turn herself slowly so as not to get too dizzy too quickly, her bare feet on the polished wood floor. This is the story of the novelist, she thought, who spun herself into the floor like a screw. She had never heard of Kafka's 'The Top'. Her stomach turned over once and she stopped, facing the wall, her head a little sore from the low pressure system moving into the city. Soon it was going to rain. Here, it is necessary for me to write this: soon it was going to rain. And then: she had too many clothes on. Necessary because it was going to rain; it did rain; she had too many clothes on. But in the space it takes to write this, how many proper stories could have been finished? Stories which could have been testimony, yes, or commentary maybe, but it wasn't ever going to rain, you know. The phone might ring, and stop her train of thought, but it wouldn't be for her. And so on that day rain never came. She stood there, naked in the sunlight which shone through her window, filling a space in which my intentions were beginning to spin.

I Went Down to the Sea

There was no reason for my arrival. No desk, no chair,
a pencil but no paper; and no obvious reason.
Maybe I'd finally fallen from grace or else just arrived,
and on arriving began to count every inch of pavement
between my feet and the water as I got closer.

In those days, not many tourists wandered the city streets,
breathing from memory, to arrive in love with the lips
of an old enemy and to sit still while the sea lapped
and laid those same lips against the pier.

That morning I was teaching myself to juggle,
in my spare time: I was handling two round stones
and a novel, between sitting and standing, sure,
and not one of them had yet touched anything but palm.

Maybe I was more clown than tourist, but at times
like this, the air heavy with humidity,
the sun is silent, will never speak, never remember,
will never leave the present tense. I am between a woman's
nude legs in a garden with a handful of flowers
I'd been juggling beforehand. Or two stones and a book.

Was it true that each day the sea, in reaching, climbs closer
and closer to the soles of my shoes? And what if the rubber
dissolves and there is nothing left but the water I started with
against bare feet? Is that why I wear socks? Sea, rubber, socks.

My dear one is watching me turn brown. The pier is my arm
against the wave of her. In my palm it's only a stone.
Stone, book, stone. What if the sea is not climbing closer?
Not because my arm is defending me, but because
it is enjoying watching me between her legs?

What a chance I had to be late, to be early for the sea's
arrival. To be a juggler of kiwi fruit or magpies.
Three, six in hand. Now I am late, now I am early.
Now I am a juggler looking into someone else's house.

Kiwi, hand, house. When I left, I left as one
who is escaping the old world to become a pilgrim
or as one who as a child joins the circus and becomes
a juggler; all my gear, my juggling things, clutched against
my chest to protect them from pickpockets and pederasts.

So it was fear that drove me home, behind the wheel
of a taxi, taking every corner away from the water
with spite and hate. 'You're all brown,' says my dear one
in her sleep while I put down my book to imagine
what my hand might hold against the hair between her legs.
A stone. A kiwi fruit. A rolled up pair of socks.

Prayer to Saint Agatha

We can affirm nothing with confidence concerning her history... As an
attribute in art her breasts, which were cut off, are often shown on a
dish... she was credited with the power of arresting the eruptions of
Mount Etna, so she is invoked against any outbreak of fire.

Butler's *Lives of the Saints*

Holy virgin of the third century,
martyr, refuter of married life,
pure thinker and resister of lechers,
I wished to write sooner, while you were young
and living among the countries of our
civilization's birth. I have every
country in mind now and every childhood,
and you are a thousand women whose breasts
have been severed because of their beliefs.
I would say something of life without you.

The kind of men you knew are gone. Women
are the same, though children may be too
serious, and we've spent most of the last
hundred years angry that our cries of 'Come
back to me,' to God and whoever,
go unanswered. No one falls asleep. Ships
sail over the desert and squirrels eat
from our hands. Taxis are yellow and films
end badly. Some of us try to hold on
to something, but there's no money in it.

I think of an apple. We have many
kinds now. Not one has given up its skin.
Not far from here, men garden and prune, trim
the lawn, and pink roses reach out to chew
the tyres off cars passing in the street.
Otherwise, we dine at the usual times
and sometimes even manage to speak
to each other. Meat and fish come frozen,
tomatoes don't taste like tomatoes, and
sandwiches are wrapped in paper and foil.

The ottoman is for feet, hair can be japanned,
noses roman. We will look the same
to you, perhaps taller, with our toes
knotted and fingers gnarled like rising
smoke. In May it rains. Sewers overflow
and spew out black tea, bits of wood, and lost
youths – the latter an army of millions
thought killed during the year's first snowfall.
On quiet mornings, you hear them calling
from the rivers running through the city.

And you, we lost track of you years ago.
Your skin must have hardened and dried, your bones
rotted through. There are images found in books,
hidden from air and outdoors; there are poems,
but not one of the words is your own.
A letter in a local magazine read,
'After reading this book I cried,' and I
recognized you in it, though left unsigned.
And still today, as you rest your head on sleep's
shoulder, you must be the broad orange sun.

Martyr and holy virgin who shunned
the breath of living men in her ear, you are
a light shining through our dark sleep. I lay
my heart open to light. I wake at dawn
thinking of warm days and the sadness here
that will last forever. Nothing could be
forgotten. The people you never met
are growing older, they cannot change now.
I make this prayer to you on their behalf:
Please rid the world once and for all of fire.

For One Whose Name God Knows

Υπέρ ευχής ου οίδεν ο θεός το όνομα

Dear to all someones and all Salonica
is Saint Demetrios, whose relics,
a chlamys, spear and shield, are lost;
a sheathed sword, as well, is nowhere found
and yet all four glow and breathe fire
in the God-loving city's churches. Fearless
by nature, he guards the streets unarmed
and heals the faithful of illness, appearing
first in dream and hidden behind a voice,
his footsteps perfuming the hollow earth.

I make not one word of this up, for he,
victorious one of Christ, is also
dear to me, as you who listen are,
who read and know this is written to you.
The curse of an erotic century
is lifting. Whenever I think of you
looking down on these words, soldiers every
one of you, I think of Demetrios,
too, whispering, *Let Salonica fall,*
in God's bitter ear in fourteen-thirty.

You make me bitter. More and more I've learned
to do without those beloved things you
are reading for, you who were made for joy.
Saint Demetrios is my example,
he who killed a scorpion with the sign
of the cross, patron of gladiators,
soldiers and the city Salonica.
Be done with your faintheartedness and
your disbelief, my soldiers. From behind
the stars, a new abandonment awaits.

Lines Attributed to Michael Psellus Concerning the Deaths of Twelve Apostles

Peter was crucified upside down in Nero's world.
And Rome also watched Paul lose his head to the sword.
In Greece Luke rested peacefully in the end.
While Matthew sleeps the sleep of a living clergyman.
Alexandrian pagans caught Mark's last breath.
And John did not die in his life and death.
Men of Patras bound Andrew to his cross.
And in India a Brahmin speared Thomas.
Bartholomew was flayed in Armenia.
The cross took Simon in Abkhazia.
In Jerusalem a blade cut Jacob's journey short.
And in Hierapolis – like Peter – Philip went to meet his Lord.

Constantine and Arete: an autobiography

Ὅλα τα λόγια που είχανε μοναδικό τους προορισμόν Ἐσένα!

Οδυσσέας Ελύτης

[*All the words that had a lonely end in you.*

Odysseas Elytis]

1

'My bags are not packed,' Constantine said,
  'and all my maps to stars' homes are aflame.'
More difficult to recognize, he'd lost
  all the sad etcetera of the wrong
and his toothbrush changing planes at Luton.
  But I sent him on, at a bus depot,
where even swallows lay down their feathers
  in protest. Turning away, I imagined
him as underdressed as those swallows –
  his birthday suit torn at neck, knee, elbow.
The time was right to break. For Arete,
  daughter of the old world, he would thrive
in travel – erecting a barricade
  of luggage in the bus toilet to sleep
his way through Shawinigan for instance –
  and my only concern was Arete.
Where to find her, and why and how and when,
  came later, along with understanding
my weakness for leaving nothing behind.
  Today, at her door, a green milk-crate
full of Northern Soul records in his arms,
  some roses and their phantoms in his teeth,
she welcomed him in and out of the rain,
  both of them slowing just enough to rest.

On the road as they walked along, birds sang,
　　though not like birds at all, not like swallows,
they sang and spoke with near-human voices:
　　Who else saw that girl following a dead man.
'Did you hear what the birds said, Constantine?'
　　'So, birds are birds – they sing; they're birds – they speak.'
Isn't it shameful, and wrong, and odd
　　for the living to wander with the dead?
'Did you hear what the birds said, Constantine,
　　about the living wandering with the dead?'
'It's April – they're warbling; May – they're nesting.'
　　'Why is it, Constantine, you smell of incense?'
'Last night we were late getting to Saint John,
　　that priest incensed us both with too much incense.'
Along they went, and soon other birds sang:
　　Look at the world's miracles and horrors,
how a lissom girl can follow a dead man!
　　When Arete heard this, her heart fissured.
'Did you hear what the birds said, Constantine?'
　　'Oh leave the birds and all, they say what they like.'
'Then tell me something: why are you so pale?
　　where is your ambition, your hair and beard?'
'There was a time I was near-death, remember,
　　and all of that and much more disappeared.'

3

Barbarian waves of barbarian hordes
　　cross the desert, where only a servant
and child of theology waves them past.
　　Arete enters her closet to pray,
calls on the Hellenes of old to balance
　　some inner and outer wisdom. For her,
everyone is cheerful as everything
　　vanishes backwards, infamous daughter
of a goatherd and a restaurateur,
　　a televangelist and Telecaster,
a hero and has-been. She is perfect
　　as the heavenly father is perfect,
seen waving from God's door – the thick dust of it.
　　So Constantine found her. Now look at him.
The desert darkens under men's shadows.
　　With doves' wings on, with mercenaries' ears
at her lips, he found her in Canada,
　　away from family, from the cold, from me.

Constantine describes a dream to Arete:
  'It was there you slept, and while sleeping dreamed
deliriously of your childhood bed,
  single, unmade. You always were like this,
living without forgetting. Hmm. Trying.
  The archangel Michael arrived in stride,
his arms akimbo. You heard him speaking:
  You've written lines and lines without any
irritable hankering after fact
  or logic. Now? I give up. I'm afraid.
I don't know if you're a tragedian
  or surrealist. I don't know. And no one
is there to find you in Etobicoke,
  where nothing waits but dead books on dead shelves.
But what the archangel actually said,
  Be happy, was interrupted by my
early-morning tapping at your window.'
  It was a wish and a counterwish on
Constantine's part, desperate, vatic. Painted
  inside him, her image, for a moment,
Mother, Mary Mother, he could believe
  in God without loving Him, but could
he love without believing? The archangel
  shook his finger, vanished; Constantine
stood up like a bolt of lightning, dumbstruck:
  'O my sweet springtime, let's just get away.'

Her paternal great-grandfather once mined
   the coal seams of upstate Pennsylvania,
a lefty and illegal migrant,
   who unionized before deportation
and screening by federal agencies
   found him in Toronto. There he gathered
his riches and left to build a rail-line
   between Salonica and Florina,
transporting hens along private iron tracks.
   It's a story Arete doesn't know
I know. And too far back for Constantine
   who as a child longed for music, vinyl,
like Myron's Marsyas, flute at his feet,
   Arete in Athene's guise. Myron,
a sculptor whose figures pointed forwards
   so that anyone might follow to the past.
I see them together, now, like statues,
   Constantine and Arete, guarding
the finished world. So it's not important
   from where they've come or for what they're reaching.

Scene six, inside the British Museum:
  'I wish to speak,' said Arete. She had
tied her hair back for the occasion.
  Visitors to the Reading Room took long breaths
while Constantine pushed through them to get away.
  Her speech began, 'The most pure Virgin saw me,
Word of God, lying supine…' But Constantine
  was out and headed towards that basalt beast,
Hoa Hakananai'a, *ex situ*,
  in the Pacific Collection. A few words
came to him there and he paused to recite them,
  standing alone before the wrong idol:
'The sky as my judge, I swore to bring her back,
  sorrow, joy or sickness. But you'd find legs
to lose her if you could.' And then Arete,
  acting as doyenne and world historian,
led her group to the hall. 'The divide between
  east and west is violent,' she told them.
Oh, here we go, so north and south are one then?
  Constantine thought, as if her inattention
to detail was weakness, and his focus
  on some sacred icon's thin, pursed lip was strength.

'My golden-branched cypress, you hear me say,
   I'm on the road to you, in Ha Giang,
where the emperor's grass grows tall as trees.
   But that's not right, because I'm in England,
I'm sure as rain falling amid the leaves.
   O terrible simplificateur, I'm not wrong,
on the road as I was coming two thieves
   took my life – Constantine too distracted –
and now I'm everywhere at once.
   Can see you my hair, streams of spider-silk,
in Ha Long Bay, where I lived the lives of ships?
   My hair fell out fighting death's currents.
And my pallor and my eyes? My stained teeth?
   Well, let me explain what isn't explained.
Like Constantine, I've been there and back,
   the shameful and wrong and strange are with me.
May we receive postcards from each other,
   my cypress, accidentally, forever.'

Mountains and fields are boundless and blessed,
    for neither welcome nor drive away death –
only sheep in summer, snow in winter.
    In the afterworld, Arete stopped three men
from returning to earth: the first in spring,
    the second, summer, and the third, autumn,
when grapes ripen. Her arms crossed, she called to each:
    'Gentleman, take me to the upper world.'
'Beautiful, I can't, don't you know I can't?
    Your clothes carry sound, your hair reflects light,
your heels clatter and old death will find us.'
    'But I'll take off my clothes, clip back my hair,
and these shit shoes can go in the fire.
    Take me, gentleman, to the upper world,
to the side of my mother in mourning.'
    'Oh, baby, your mother's rambling in the streets.'
'To the side of my father in mourning.'
    'Honey, your father's drinking in a bar.'
'To my brother and sister in mourning.'
    'Lady, your siblings are living their lives.'
'To the homes of my cousins in mourning.'
    'Lover, your cousins are dancing the dance.'

The earth rings the bells, the sky rings the bells,
   God rings the bells, returns the dead to life.
There they were in the seven-hilled city,
   Constantine and Arete, when he said:
'Have you heard this one? May twenty-ninth,
   Tuesday, fourteen-fifty-three, a monk
in Constantinople was frying fish
   when told that after a two-month siege
the walls had fallen; the Church of the Holy
   Wisdom had been claimed for Islam by
Mehmet the Conqueror – who had showered
   earth on his turbaned head before entering.
The City was overrun with Turks, but
   the priest replied this was as likely
as his half-cooked fish jumping from its pan
   into the nearby spring. The fish then did.'
The faithful are travellers swimming
   in holy springs, less careful of each other
than fish, less kind. May twenty-eighth, fourteen-
   fifty-three, the bells in Hagia Sofia ring:
four-hundred sounding boards, sixty-two bells.
   One day later, a fish returns to life.
'Is it so unbelievable, after
   all these deaths and lives, I am yours today?'
They are less careful of each other, where
   in time understanding should grow, less kind.

Dear Constantine, are we just hypocrites,
   singing songs with music above the words?
Speaking of things can be horrible too.
   One night I was looking at her dimly-lit
body when woken by a kind of singing
   that consoles, an expression of inner
necessity. And then, when I think
   I've understood, a solitary voice
can change everything: dream's clumsy hand
   seems less threatening, slips from time to time.
Two songs later, a miracle occurs:
   somewhere Sigur Rós sing 'Hoppípolla',
Thelma Houston sings 'Jumpin' Jack Flash'.
   There is more good to come yet, miracle,
no need to descend to the literal,
   moral or supernatural meanings
of the world. Whatever your role, teach me.
   'It is not wrong to be victorious,'
Constantine wrote back, from their Spanish flat,
   and I suppose, while spinning a piece
of rose quartz on the table, it isn't,
   'and stop assuming I'm an allegory.'

My black swallows from within the desert
  and my white doves from closer to the coast,
should you fly anywhere near my home
  you'll see an apple tree in the front yard;
if you land, could you tell my mother
  if she wants to become a nun, to retreat,
if she wants to dye her clothes black in mourning,
  she shouldn't wait any longer. Here, in
Armenia, they've married me to
  a witch's daughter, an Armenian taken
to be my young wife, who casts spells
  over the skies and stars, casts spells over
fish and stops them swimming, casts spells
  over rivers and stops them flowing,
over the sea she casts spells and waves stop breaking,
  she casts spells over boats so they stop sailing,
casts spells over me and I stop running.
  If I set out for home, snow and rain,
and when I turn back, sun and clear skies.
  I saddle my horse, it comes unsaddled,
I buckle my sword to my belt, it unfastens,
  I take paper to write but the sheet stays clean.

Four a.m.: the phone rang and someone
    grumbled softly, 'That's enough. I've had enough,'
then stepped onto a plane bound for Tokyo.
    Not hiding his erection, Constantine
opened the door. 'Do you like Baudelaire?'
    she asked, unpacking a handmade tea set
and a military-issue compass.
    Baudelaire. He knew a song, not the poems,
wished just then to fix them all in his mind:
    Mon enfant, ma soeur, songe à la douceur,
he recited, *D'aller là-bas, vivre ensemble.*
    And his ambition was very proud, looked
down from above and longed to sift through her
    luggage. But many times, it's the jumping
bean not the larvae inside that attracts.
    Jumping bean. It is not for her, little
one, that I write this down from memory,
    though memory explains how it happened.
'Honey child, don't you want to buy a house?
    Know what? No. What you said. In French.
Whatever you said.' Their life together:
    one of them the paintings hanging in the
living room, the other the storm windows.
    A different suffering gripping both.

Stubbornly Arete repeated,
   'I desire to be free from marriage and
invite assistance in bringing this about.'
   Her previous lover, a janissary
in the employ of Ali Effendi,
   took the news badly and slowed his heart rate
until he appeared dead to then modern
   medical methods. Arete caught on.
She attended his mock-funeral
   in a Nudie Suit and never cried once,
offering her virginity as dowry
   afterwards to our Lord Jesus Christ.
But He was well aware she sermonized
   while pointing to her crotch and winking.
Constantine managed to get his fingers
   in there once or twice while they were slowing
and O the things she stopped him from doing,
   a leg in each hand – he would surprise her when
his lips found bare breasts or her little stomach.
   She never let anyone play with her breasts.
The janissary burned or buried alive,
   God deceived and rewarded them again.

Not for the first time and not for the last,
   Constantine held Arete's arm in his hand,
cried out for Miss Rodeo Canada,
   and fell asleep in the Lord. This being
the kind of thing he liked to do, it came
   as no surprise. But a shock and a twinge
held in her muscle, like being bitten,
   diagnosed by a rheumatologist
as RSD or maybe neurosis,
   which Arete knew to be regret for the loss
of heaven, a spasm and a shudder
   meaning, 'It'll never happen again,
this world, once seemingly unified, now
   divided. With your revenant you go.'
She'd gotten as far as Glasgow when he
   rose from the dead, confused equal of Christ,
trampling death upon death, sister, brother,
   granting life to those in the tombs, insulting,
seducing, and corrupting everyone
   he could touch. Her arm ached. So many do.
'I don't blame you much for wanting to be free –,'
   she sang, in Scotland, at once confusing
Nina Simone with P.P. Arnold,
   the roar of pain gathered for its curtain call.

My moon, look down on me alone on earth.
    And you my stars, the field in which I sow,
till, rummage, and you canopy of leaves,
    ditches full of dust, the recycling bins,
street lamps, sidewalks, the gravel and wet tar:
    have you seen an unattainable man
amid the carefree women, nymphs, nymphets
    who weep and surrender, bow and scrape tongues
from their flesh? Let's send him on to hell.
    Let him climb a tree, a tall tree that bends
and let him break an arm. Let him trip crossing
    a bridge and fall like a brick to the water.
Let him end up drowned in a well. And doctors,
    if you work him over, will you write out
what he suffered? So that I can have more
    than place names and unsuitable longing.

Worm at the root, worm at the centre, worm
   of divinity, our spirit is an abyss
living in the abyss: vine and vein, life–
   line, what carries over, divine or dire.
Poor Constantine closes his eyes falling
   backwards into a pool and emerges
laughing; kisses his pillow before sleep;
   hunts the bird that tortured Prometheus.
His name is oil poured out, the fragrance
   we follow, as sorrow follows a worm
along roots to a tree. He has settled
   to stay in Florence, and so we settle.
Pisa he says he thinks and we say and think.
   Yet tonight if life is more than he is,
there'll be some relief, Arete thought.
   But no, because the world she knows little
of goes from grace to grace, and he is
   no swimmer, no narcissist, no hunter:
in the world she knows, Constantine is hunted.
   And also in my dreams he is hunted.

'Allow the saddest actress to take the stage,
   calming rippling seas of theatregoers.
You've directed me to spin, pirouette,
   but won't answer, will you, if I ask:
why can't Penelope come to war?
   won't the hero bring Andromache home?
Saying something smart and necessary
   is called for, to ease the fall of my head
onto the pillow, so that where we once
   took rest, there is the curve of eyebrow,
where we were meant to end, the arch of nostril.
   I love your face amid the ten thousand
stories of my death – in each my legs lie on
   some living room floor, a sea between knee
and ankle – the Georgian purdonium,
   the fire screen, the soundtrack by Midlake.
No, you could never be an astronaut
   nor pilot, so turn to Penelope,
to Andromache, and all that we see
   and grasp is unknowable but pleasant.
We aren't wheelchair-bound where once we slept tight.
   The sea that rippled is calm in the end.'

He, Constantine, penelopised writing
   his novel of the immigrant experience
by talking a good game over Satie,
   Lee Hazlewood and Gal Costa records:
'These days much of what we read is by chance:
   books, articles and essays written to rid
women of their melancholy. Even poems,
   especially poems, beside one another
in magazines, in some way say farewell
   and at the same time ask you to continue.
They ought to throttle everything in mind,
   but don't, and instead, livid with rage,
rush about fields breaking the heads off chanterelles.
   How about this: a poem is a bookmark
inside Pearl S. Buck's *All Men Are Brothers*.
   The bookmark reminds you you're not finished.
For, if you were to finish, your head full…'
   But he disappeared before he could go on.
It's reported, though no one knows for sure,
   that this time Zeus cast him into the clouds.

The ceremony of morning over,
  sleep washed from eyes, tea and breakfast devoured,
young Constantine scratches at his birthmark.
  He has explained it, alternately,
as stab wound, laser tattoo removal,
  and the scar from an appendectomy.
'Perfection,' he says, 'is childish, implies
  flawlessness. Perfection is perverse.'
Then he stretches out his left hand with strength
  enough to lift a mountain, and his right
hand lifts as though he would carry a child:
  a mixture of baby powder and body
odour surrounding him, he salutes
  a passerby: 'Let me just adjust your bra.'
Four hundred and twenty-one days of this,
  announcements and accusations, and still
no proof of his miraculous existence.
  'This will sound too much like an old novel,
but in the past even I could begin
  living the wrong life. For how did a man
reborn by God hide so well a mark
  received when he was raped by a waterfall –
itself disguised as a god – before
  an indifferent river could drag me on?'

Arete writes of Constantine's cruelty:
   'In Uppsala last night, dreamed he was
chasing me through a field of snowmen.
   Chasing me, that is, until he became
a jackdaw pecking at my breasts.
   I'd no choice but to seize and devour him.
Life, for awhile, went differently, though I
   never spoke of it. When a Japanese
oni, which lived only to love men, convinced
   itself no man could love it and vanished
with his child in its belly, O my Christ,
   does memory ever weigh heavy on earth.
As birds fly above, we live again, find
   some secret of the separate heart
amid the scattered topsoil he escaped
   his grave through. Memory. Or just a dream.
Linnaeus believed Gamla Uppsala
   the centre of Atlantis.' No, Rudbeck,
not Linnaeus. There's no room for mistakes.
   Two days after writing these things, she's gone.

Lord Jesus Christ, son of God, have mercy.
    At night your gift, your revenant, is not
enough – the world never just sex and death,
    there is war, too, that great recombinant,
there is sin and there is resurrection.
    At night, a voice from the sky, from the mouth
of the archangel, repeats the unknown:
    drink from my cup while the world spins and sleep.
Unknown to us, Lord, her body amid
    brambles and dead branches of bedding, open
till the end like a circle cut in glass
    by a burglar, You answered every prayer,
fulfilled every wish as the world ended.
    What I have in mind is a blue lemon
hanging on a fetid, leafless tree.
    What I have in mind there is no sense of.
Call the soldiers of heaven to guard the gates,
    star, dawn and new moon, though the war may pass.
We adventure now for the miracle,
    whose spirit is white water over falls.
At night, the light of a lamp warms the room,
    too much or too little, depending on
the season, without possibility,
    for even admirable days will end.

'Dear Evan, spoke with your parents last night,
    your sisters, the two kids, the baby, your
brother-in-law. Not one knows where you are.
    We asked too a garden in bloom, some little
birds on branches, and even the tireless moon.
    Having written this out six or seven times
since then, we hope the words will come now cleanly.
    You leave us first to God and then the saints.
.Where is your two cents? Your last word?
    Your secret sharing? If now you live in
a brick house, you must think it made of glass.
    We are cups full of water. Perhaps some
saint will swallow us, and memory, too.
    Or return to remind us endlessly
of what we don't know, because we don't.
    Soon we'd like to say, 'Hello', to you
and not, 'Goodbye', 'Forever'. There's no time
    for both. You won't hear from us again,
what is dead stays dead, what the living do remains,
    sincerely, Constantine and Arete.

The Chinese believe a lunar eclipse
   is caused by a toad living in the moon.
See how I sound more like them, welcome rain
   sprinkling the balsam of mercy over
their ashes and bones, placing a kiss
   behind their ears – did I whisper revenant
or ruminant then? They're one and the same.
   Tonight, in half-sleep, I drew up a list:
Ten things they would like me not to do,
   it began, not aiming for eloquence.
But the wanting's old, I know, Saint Hautecoeur,
   post-Byzantine patron of patience
and counting to ten – which leaves us all cold.
   So let's keep the baby, buy a house, let's
chase me while someone over-inclined towards
   sensual love who never turns his head,
never blows his nose, never once spits, rises.
   The only unattainable love safer
than God's is my own. There is, the Chinese
   are fond of saying, a poem to prove it.

One face, one voice, one habit, and two persons,
A natural perspective, that is and is not.
                    Twelfth Night, v.i.216–17

After the press conferences and cocktails,
   tales of narwhals *et autres monstres marins*,
the endless hearsay, public opinion,
   the unanswered emails and dead letters,
to let Constantine and Arete go,
   having followed them in poems, in cities,
pinpointed their locations thematically,
   destined their painful and truthful natures,
lived again with them or else alternately
   drawn nearer to bestiaries overfull
of *les figures humaines* (who are either
   inaccessible mistresses, heavenly
objects or incarnations of desire).
   Translating folklore into myth, the common
story of life, they went along together,
   returning as one, burning whole countries
they visited until all that remained
   was people they knew and had finished with.
Where they went I can't go: the only things
   that die are those that want to be dead,
but no one comes down from the cross alive.
   Yet in my next poem, this may not be so.

Note

'Constantine and Arete' takes as its starting point a number of medieval Greek folk poems, most prominent of which is 'Το Τραγούδι του Νεκρού Αδερψού' [The Song of the Dead Brother]. These poem are knowns as παραλογές [ballads], a genre word whose etymology links it to the illogical, the supernatural, things that are 'beyond the logos', beyond the word of God. The narrative tells of a young man, Constantine, who arranges with matchmakers from Babylon a marriage for his only sister and then, along with his eight brothers, dies of the plague. Left alone and dying herself, their mother summons Constantine from the dead to bring Arete back to her. He obliges and sets off. Arete, in her new home, unaware of what has happened, is convinced to return. Their journey is strange, and Arete knows that Constantine is not himself. Arriving at their family home, Constantine disappears; Arete is reunited with her mother, and both die.